SCOTT FORESMAN
READING STREET

KINDERGARTEN

COMMON CORE

Program Authors

Peter Afflerbach
Camille Blachowicz
Candy Dawson Boyd
Elena Izquierdo
Connie Juel
Edward Kame'enui
Donald Leu
Jeanne R. Paratore

P. David Pearson
Sam Sebesta
Deborah Simmons
Susan Watts Taffe
Alfred Tatum
Sharon Vaughn
Karen Kring Wixson

SAVVAS
LEARNING COMPANY

*We dedicate Reading Street to
Peter Jovanovich.*

*His wisdom, courage,
and passion for education
are an inspiration to us all.*

RENAISSANCE
Accelerated Reader

Copyright © 2013 by Savvas Learning Company LLC. All Rights Reserved. Printed in the United States of America.

This publication is protected by copyright, and permission should be obtained from the publisher prior to any prohibited reproduction, storage in a retrieval system, or transmission in any form or by any means, electronic, mechanical, photocopying, recording, or otherwise. For information regarding permissions, request forms, and the appropriate contacts within the Savvas Learning Company Rights Management group, please send your query to the address below.

Savvas Learning Company LLC, 15 East Midland Avenue, Paramus, NJ 07652

Attributions of third party content appear on page 144, which constitutes an extension of this copyright page.

Common Core State Standards: © Copyright 2010. National Governors Association Center for Best Practices and Council of Chief State School Officers. All rights reserved.

Savvas™ and **Savvas Learning Company™** are the exclusive trademarks of Savvas Learning Company LLC in the U.S. and other countries.

Savvas Learning Company publishes through its famous imprints **Prentice Hall®** and **Scott Foresman®** which are exclusive registered trademarks owned by Savvas Learning Company LLC in the U.S. and/or other countries.

Reading Street® and **Savvas Realize™** are exclusive trademarks of Savvas Learning Company LLC in the U.S. and/or other countries.

Unless otherwise indicated herein, any third party trademarks that may appear in this work are the property of their respective owners, and any references to third party trademarks, logos, or other trade dress are for demonstrative or descriptive purposes only. Such references are not intended to imply any sponsorship, endorsement, authorization, or promotion of Savvas Learning Company products by the owners of such marks, or any relationship between the owner and Savvas Learning Company LLC or its authors, licensees, or distributors.

ISBN-13: 978-1-428-47358-4
ISBN-10:　　1-428-47358-0

Dear Reader,

Wow! School has started! Did you know that we are about to take a trip along Reading Street? AlphaBuddy and your very own book, *My Skills Buddy,* will be with you for the whole trip.

Let's get ready. Pack your thinking caps. On Reading Street we will be busy learning to read and write and think. It will be hard work, but it will be fun.

You will meet lots of interesting characters. We'll make a stop in Trucktown too.

As AlphaBuddy likes to say, "Let's get this show on the road!"

Sincerely,
The Authors

Unit 1 Contents

All Together Now

 How do we live, work, and play together?

Week 1

Let's Listen for Rhyming Words 12

Comprehension: Literary Elements 14

Print Awareness and High-Frequency Words 16

I Can Read! Decodable Reader 1
  Who Am I? 18

Animal Fantasy • Social Studies
The Little School Bus by Carol Roth
Retell/Think, Talk, and Write 26

Big Book

Let's Learn It! 28

Let's Practice It! **Myth** 30

4

Week 2

Let's Listen for Syllables 32

Comprehension: Literary Elements 34

Print Awareness and High-Frequency Words 36

I Can Read! Decodable Reader 2
Am I? 38

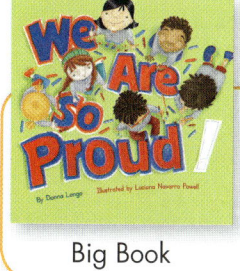
Big Book

Realistic Fiction • Social Studies
We Are So Proud! by Donna Longo

Retell/Think, Talk, and Write 46

Let's Learn It! 48

Let's Practice It! Expository Text 50

Unit 1 Contents

Week 3

Let's Listen for Initial Sounds 52

Comprehension: Sequence 54

Print Awareness and High-Frequency Words 56

I Can Read! Decodable Reader 3

The Little Toys 58

Realistic Fiction • Social Studies

Plaidypus Lost
by Janet Stevens and Susan Stevens Crummel

Retell/Think, Talk, and Write 66

Big Book

Let's Learn It! 68

Let's Practice It! Fable 70

Week 4

Let's Listen for Initial Sounds 72

Comprehension: Classify and Categorize 74

Print Awareness and High-Frequency Words 76

I Can Read! Decodable Reader 4

At the Zoo 78

Animal Fantasy • Social Studies

Miss Bindergarten Takes a Field Trip with Kindergarten by Joseph Slate

Retell/Think, Talk, and Write 86

Big Book

Let's Learn It! 88

Let's Practice It! Recipe 90

Week 5

Let's Listen for Initial Sounds 92

Comprehension: Literary Elements 94

Print Awareness and High-Frequency Words . . . 96

I Can Read! Decodable Reader 5

Animal Friends 98

Big Book

Fantasy • Social Studies
Smash! Crash! by Jon Scieszka

Retell/Think, Talk, and Write 106

Let's Learn It! 108

Let's Practice It! **Signs** 110

Week 6

Let's Listen for Initial Sounds 112

Comprehension: Classify and Categorize 114

Phonics and High-Frequency Words 116

I Can Read! Decodable Reader 6

Let's Go 118

Big Book

Nonfiction • Science
Dig Dig Digging by Margaret Mayo

Retell/Think, Talk, and Write 126

Let's Learn It! 128

Let's Practice It! **Folk Tale** 130

READING STREET   The Digital Path!

Don Leu
The Internet Guy

Right before our eyes, the nature of reading and learning is changing. The Internet and other technologies create new opportunities, new solutions, and new literacies. New reading comprehension skills are required online. They are increasingly important to our students and our society.

Those of us on the Reading Street team are here to help you on this new, and very exciting, journey.

See It!

- Big Question Video
- Concept Talk Video
- Envision It! Animations
- eReaders

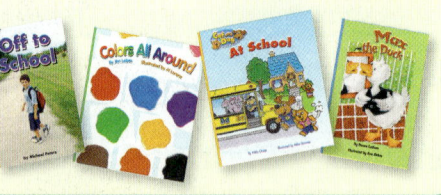

Hear It!

- *Sing with Me* Animations
- eSelections
- Grammar Jammer

Adam and Kim play at the beach.

Concept Talk Video

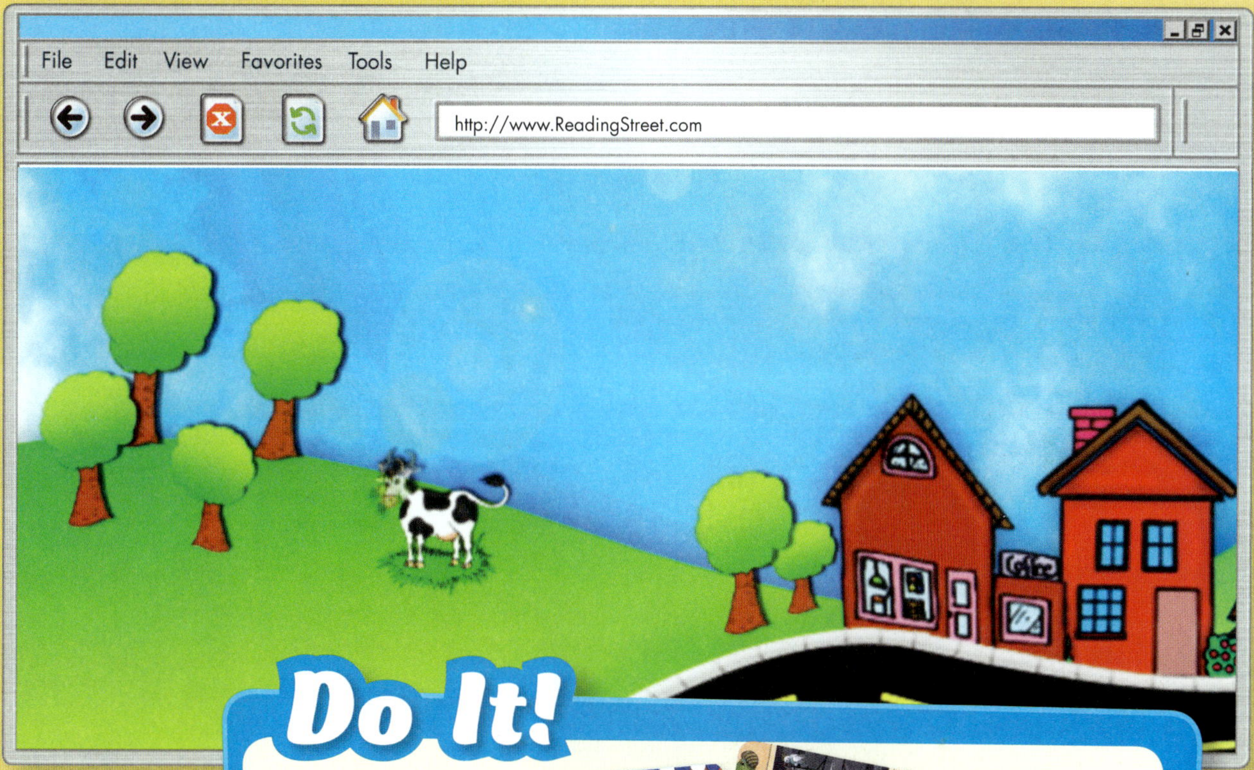

Do It!

- Story Sort 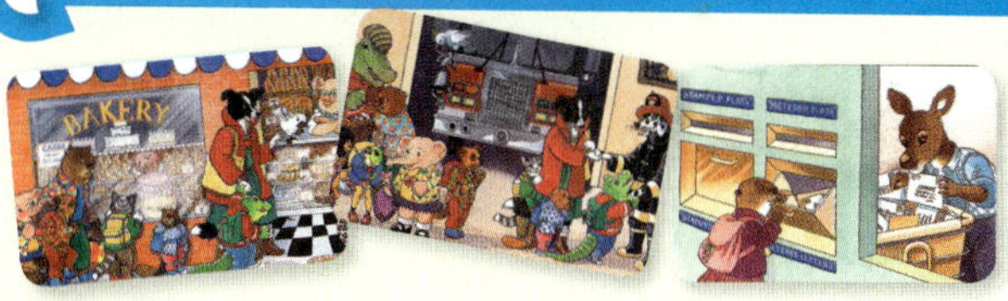
- eReaders 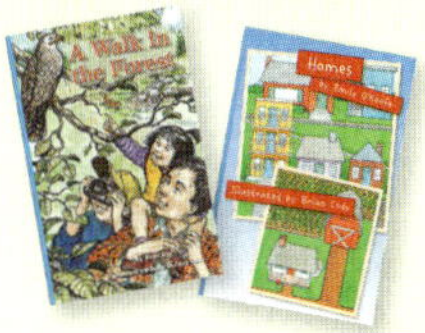
- Letter Tile Drag and Drop

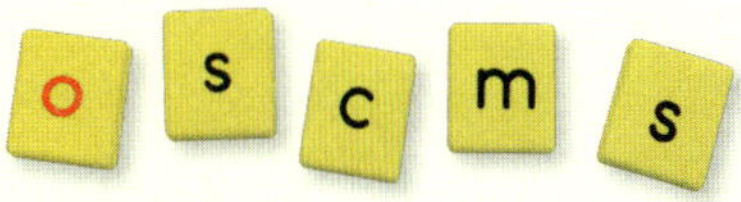

Common Core State Standards
Foundational Skills 2.a. Recognize and produce rhyming words.

Phonological Awareness

Let's Listen for

Rhyming Words

- Find things that rhyme.
- What rhymes with *man*? with *mop*? with *coat*? with *book*?
- Which word pairs rhyme: *nap/lap*, *cook/coat*, *boat/goat*?

Read Together

READING STREET ONLINE
BIG QUESTION VIDEO
www.ReadingStreet.com

12

Plot

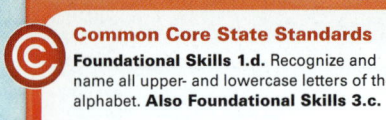

Common Core State Standards
Foundational Skills 1.d. Recognize and name all upper- and lowercase letters of the alphabet. **Also Foundational Skills 3.c.**

Print Awareness
Letter Recognition

Letters I Know

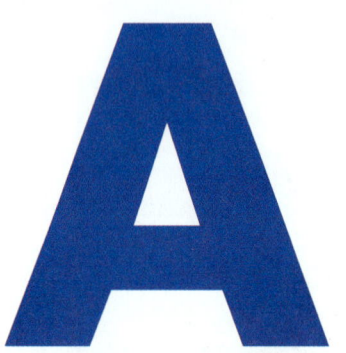

High-Frequency Words

Words I Can Read

I

am

Sentences I Can Read

1. I am  .

2. I am  .

Common Core State Standards
Foundational Skills 4. Read emergent-reader texts with purpose and understanding.
Also Foundational Skills 1.a., 1.d., 3.c.

Phonics

Decodable Reader

- Letter Recognition
  Aa
  Bb
  Cc
  Dd
  Ee
- High-Frequency Words
  I
  am
▲ Read the story.

READING STREET ONLINE
DECODABLE eREADERS
www.ReadingStreet.com

Who Am I?

Written by Bob Atkins
Illustrated by Yvette Pierre

Decodable Reader 1

18

I am Ann.

I am Ben.

I am Cam.

I am Dot.

I am Ed.

I am Emma.

I am Dad.

Think, Talk, and Write

1. How do you get to school? *Text to Self*

2. Which is a character from *The Little School Bus*? *Character*

3. Look back and write.

Common Core State Standards
Speaking/Listening 1.a. Follow agreed-upon rules for discussions (e.g., listening to others and taking turns speaking about the topics and texts under discussion).
Also Language 6.

Let's Learn It!

Vocabulary
- Talk about the pictures.
- Which do you use?

Listening and Speaking
- Point to the picture of the bus.
- Cover the picture of the bus with your hand.
- Pretend to drive a bus.

Vocabulary

Words for Transportation

bus

car

van

bike

28

Listening and Speaking

Follow Directions

Be a good listener!

29

Common Core State Standards

Speaking/Listening 2. Confirm understanding of a text read aloud or information presented orally or through other media by asking and answering questions about key details and requesting clarification if something is not understood. **Also Literature 3.**

Let's Practice It!

Myth

- Listen to the myth.
- How does it begin?
- Who is King Midas?
- How does King Midas get the "golden touch"?
- What lesson does King Midas learn?

King Midas and the Golden Touch

30

Common Core State Standards
Literature 3. With prompting and support, identify characters, settings, and major events in a story.

Comprehension

Envision It!

Literary Elements

READING STREET ONLINE
ENVISION IT! ANIMATIONS
www.ReadingStreet.com

Characters

Setting

34

Plot

Common Core State Standards
Foundational Skills 1.d. Recognize and name all upper- and lowercase letters of the alphabet.
Also Foundational Skills 1.b., 3.c.

Envision It! Letters to Know

READING STREET ONLINE
ALPHABET CARDS
www.ReadingStreet.com

Print Awareness

Letter Recognition

Letters I Know

Cc Dd Ee

Ff Gg Hh

Ii

cab

The cab is yellow.

36

High-Frequency Words

Words I Can Read

Sentences I Can Read

1. I am .

2. Am I ?

Common Core State Standards
Foundational Skills 1.a. Follow words from left to right, top to bottom, and page by page.
Also Foundational Skills 1.d., 3.c., 4.

Phonics

Decodable Reader

- Letter Recognition
  Ff
  Gg
  Hh
  Ii
  Jj
  Kk
  Ll
- High-Frequency Words
  I
  am
- Read the story.

**READING STREET ONLINE
DECODABLE eREADERS**
www.ReadingStreet.com

Am I?

Written by George Helm
Illustrated by Tori Wheaton

Decodable Reader 2

I am Jan.

Am I Fran?

I am Len.

Am I Ken?

I am Kim.

Am I Hanna?

I am Gus.

Think, Talk, and Write

1. How do we work and play together? **Text to Self**

2. Where does the story *We Are So Proud!* take place?

 Setting

3. Look back and write.

Common Core State Standards
Language 5.a. Sort common objects into categories (e.g., shapes, foods) to gain a sense of the concepts the categories represent. **Also Literature 1., Speaking/Listening 1.a., Language 6.**

Vocabulary

- 🔵 What do you see that is red?
- 🟪 What do you see that is white?
- 🔺 What do you see that is blue?

Listening and Speaking

- 🔵 Where does the story take place?
- 🟪 What is your favorite part of the story? Why?
- 🔺 Who is your favorite character in the story? Why?

Vocabulary

Color Words

red

white

blue

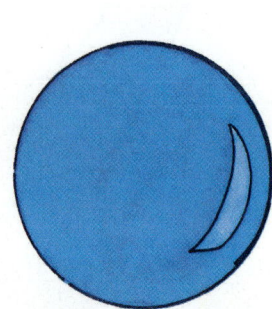

Listening and Speaking

Respond to Literature
Drama

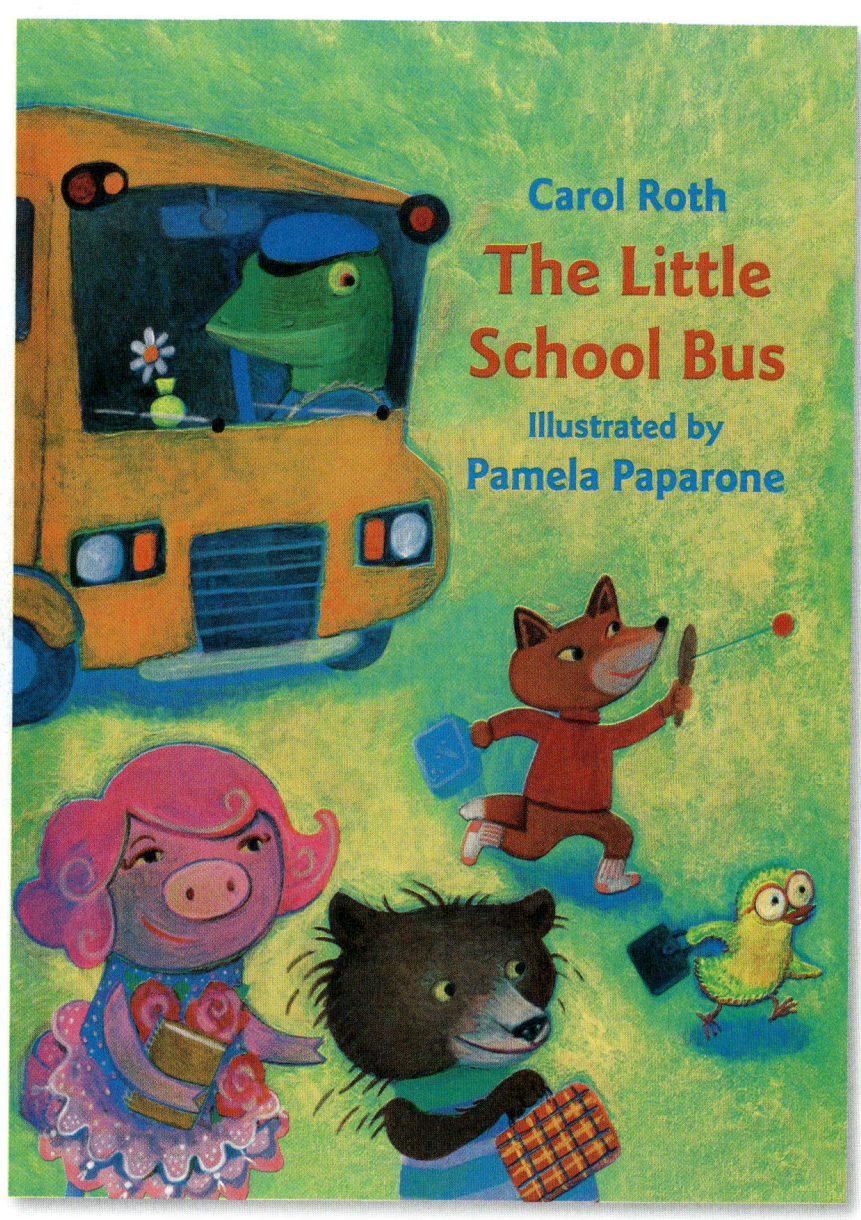

Be a good speaker!

Common Core State Standards
Speaking/Listening 2. Confirm understanding of a text read aloud or information presented orally or through other media by asking and answering questions about key details and requesting clarification if something is not understood.
Also Informational Text 1., 2., 3., 7.

Let's Practice It!

Expository Text

- Listen to the selection.
- What is this selection about?
- How are the two flags alike? How are they different?
- Why does the U.S. flag have 13 stripes?
- What do the 50 stars on the U.S. flag stand for?

The United States Flag

U.S. Flag Today

First U.S. Flag

Common Core State Standards
Literature 2. With prompting and support, retell familiar stories, including key details. **Also Literature 3.**

Comprehension

Envision It!
Sequence

READING STREET ONLINE
ENVISION IT! ANIMATIONS
www.ReadingStreet.com

Common Core State Standards
Foundational Skills 1.d. Recognize and name all upper- and lowercase letters of the alphabet.
Also Foundational Skills 1.b., 3.c.

Envision It! Letters to Know

Print Awareness

Letter Recognition

Letters I Know

Jj Kk Ll

Mm Nn

Oo Pp

mop

The mop is wet.

56

High-Frequency Words

Words I Can Read

| the |

| little |

Sentences I Can Read

1. I am little.

2. I am the little 🐕.

57

Common Core State Standards
Foundational Skills 4. Read emergent-reader texts with purpose and understanding.
Also Foundational Skills 1.a., 1.d., 3.c.

Phonics

Decodable Reader

- Letter Recognition
  Mm
  Nn
  Oo
  Pp
  Qq
  Rr
  Ss
- High-Frequency Words
  I
  am
  the
  little
▲ Read the story.

READING STREET ONLINE
DECODABLE eREADERS
www.ReadingStreet.com

The Little Toys

Written by Roger Jons
Illustrated by Scott Salinski

Decodable Reader 3

58

I am the little robot.

I am the little puzzle.

I am the little queen.

I am the little octopus.

I am the little train.

I am the little block.

I am the little spaceship.

Think, Talk, and Write

1. How do you help your family? **Text to Self**

2. What happens first in the story? What happens last?

Sequence

3. Look back and write.

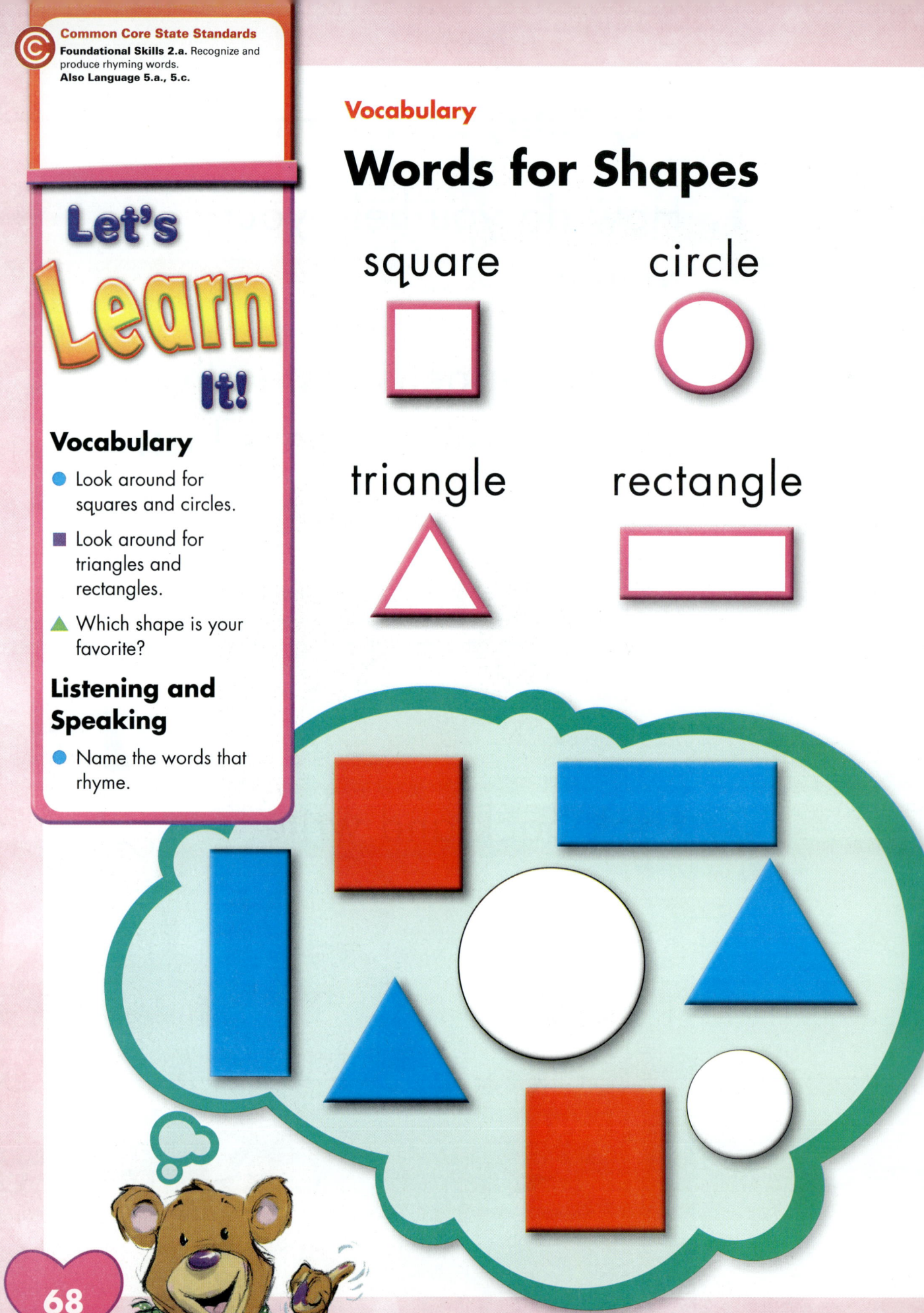

Listening and Speaking

Listen for Rhyme and Rhythm

Be a good listener!

Common Core State Standards

Speaking/Listening 2. Confirm understanding of a text read aloud or information presented orally or through other media by asking and answering questions about key details and requesting clarification if something is not understood.
Also Literature 1., 3., 5.

Let's Practice It!

The Boy Who Cried Wolf!

Fable

- Listen to the fable.
- Why does the shepherd boy cry "Wolf!" the first two times?
- What lesson does the shepherd boy learn? Has anything like this ever happened to you? Tell about it.
- What do you think the shepherd boy might do next?
- A moral is a lesson learned. What new expression does this fable teach you?

70

71

Common Core State Standards
Foundational Skills 2.d. Isolate and pronounce the initial, medial vowel, and final sounds (phonemes) in three-phoneme (consonant-vowel-consonant, or CVC) words. **Also Foundational Skills 2.e.**

Phonemic Awareness

Let's Listen for

Initial Sounds

- Point to the pig in the puddle. Say "a pig in a puddle." What sound do you hear repeated?

- Point to the man with the mouse. Say "a man with a mouse." What sound is repeated?

- Find things that begin with /b/, /d/, /k/, /p/, and /m/.

- Name two things that begin like *ball*, *desk*, *key*, *pen*, and *met*.

READING STREET ONLINE
BIG QUESTION VIDEO
www.ReadingStreet.com

72

Common Core State Standards
Language 5.a. Sort common objects into categories (e.g., shapes, foods) to gain a sense of the concepts the categories represent.

Comprehension

Envision It!
Classify and Categorize

READING STREET ONLINE
ENVISION IT! ANIMATIONS
www.ReadingStreet.com

Print Awareness

Letter Recognition

Letters I Know

Q q   R r   S s

T t   U u   V v

sun

The sun is hot.

High-Frequency Words

Words I Can Read

the

little

Sentences I Can Read

1. Am I little?

2. I am the little .

Common Core State Standards
Foundational Skills 4. Read emergent-reader texts with purpose and understanding.
Also Foundational Skills 1.d., 3.c.

Phonics

Decodable Reader

- Letter Recognition
  Tt
  Uu
  Vv
  Ww
  Xx
  Yy
  Zz

- High-Frequency Words
  I
  am
  the
  little

▲ Read the story.

READING STREET ONLINE
DECODABLE eREADERS
www.ReadingStreet.com

At the Zoo

Written by Nitty Jones
Illustrated by Amy Sparks

Decodable Reader 4

I am the little walrus.

I am the little tiger.

I am the little yak.

I am the little ox.

I am the little rhino.

I am the little zebra.

I am the little umbrella bird.

Think, Talk, and Write

1. Who helps in our town?

Text to World

2. Which things belong together?

Classify and Categorize

3. Look back and write.

Common Core State Standards
Speaking/Listening 4. Describe familiar people, places, things, and events and, with prompting and support, provide additional detail. Also Speaking/Listening 1.a., Language 6.

Vocabulary
- Talk about the pictures.
- Where do you go in your neighborhood?

Listening and Speaking
- What is your favorite color? Why do you like it?

Vocabulary
Location Words

library

park

school

post office

Listening and Speaking

Tell About Me

Be a good speaker!

Curry Veggie Dip

Step 1

Let's Practice It!

Recipe

- Listen to the recipe.
- What is the third step in the recipe?
- Which words in the recipe name actions for you to do?
- Why do people read recipes?

Common Core State Standards
Informational Text 1. With prompting and support, ask and answer questions about key details in a text.
Also Speaking/Listening 2.

Step 2

Step 3

Step 4

Common Core State Standards
Foundational Skills 2.d. Isolate and pronounce the initial, medial vowel, and final sounds (phonemes) in three-phoneme (consonant-vowel-consonant, or CVC) words. Also Foundational Skills 2.e.

Phonemic Awareness

Let's Listen for

Initial Sounds

- Point to the man in the ticket booth. Say "Man makes money." What sound do you hear at the beginning of those words?

- Find three things in the picture that begin with /m/.

- Name other words that begin with /m/.

**READING STREET ONLINE
BIG QUESTION VIDEO**
www.ReadingStreet.com

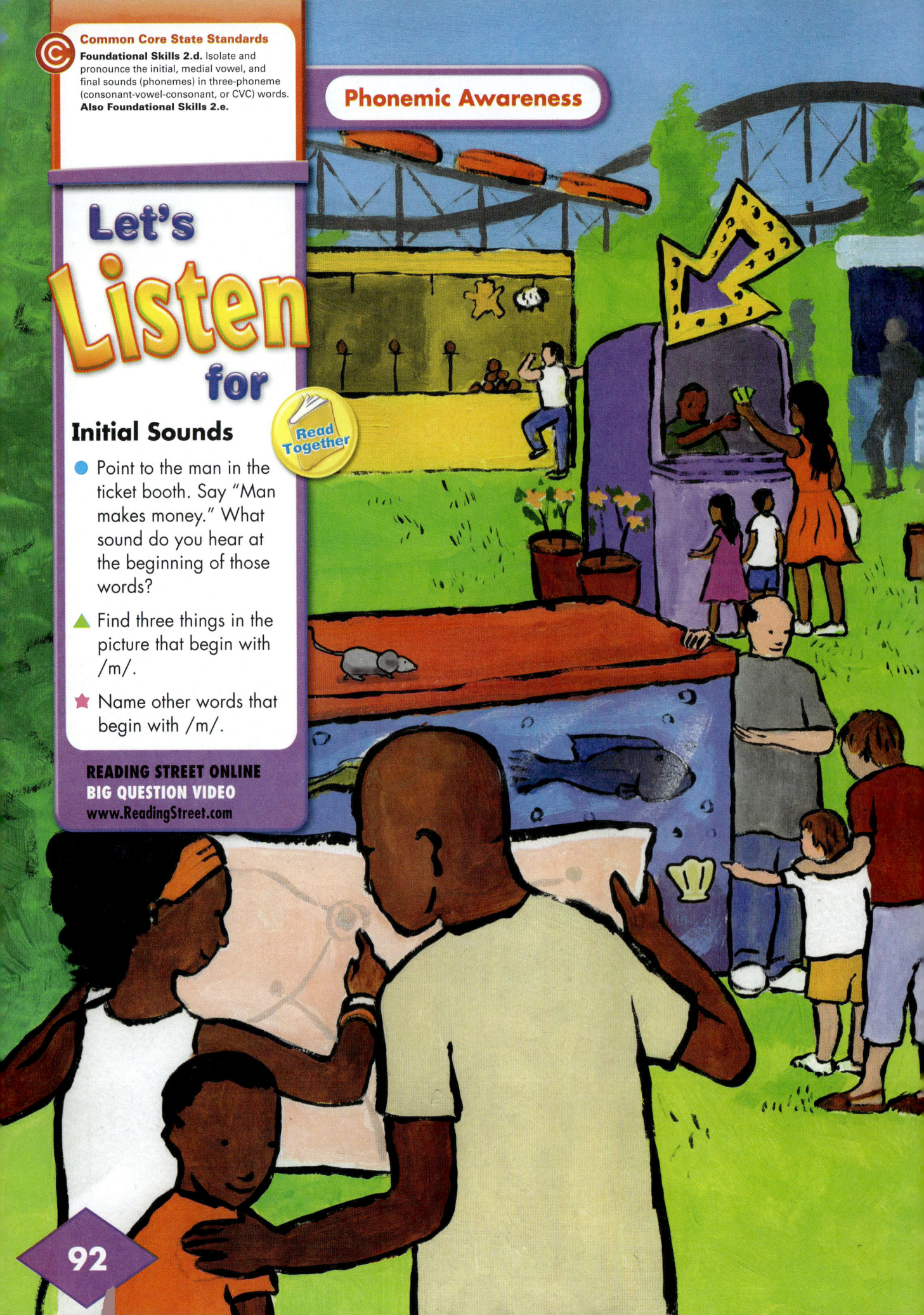

Common Core State Standards

Literature 3. With prompting and support, identify characters, settings, and major events in a story.

Comprehension

Envision It!

Literary Elements

READING STREET ONLINE
ENVISION IT! ANIMATION
www.ReadingStreet.com

Characters

Setting

Plot

Common Core State Standards
Foundational Skills 1.d. Recognize and name all upper- and lowercase letters of the alphabet.
Also Foundational Skills 2.d., 3.c.

Envision It! Letters to Know

watermelon

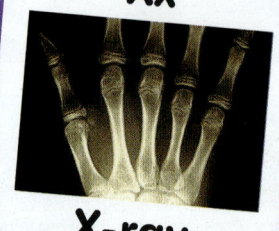
X-ray

yo-yo

zigzag

**READING STREET ONLINE
ALPHABET CARDS**
www.ReadingStreet.com

Print Awareness
Letter Recognition

Letters I Know

W w   X x

Y y   Z z

fox

The fox is red.

High-Frequency Words

Words I Can Read

to

a

Sentences I Can Read

1. I am a  .

2. I  to a .

Common Core State Standards
Foundational Skills 4. Read emergent-reader texts with purpose and understanding.
Also Foundational Skills 1.d., 3.c.

Phonics

Decodable Reader

- Consonant Mm (with rebus)
  monkey
  mule
  mouse
  minnow
  moth
  mole
  moose

- High-Frequency Words
  I
  am
  a
  little

- Read the story.

**READING STREET ONLINE
DECODABLE eREADERS**
www.ReadingStreet.com

Animal Friends

Written by Phil Morton
Illustrated by Julie Word

Decodable Reader 5

I am a little monkey.

I am a little mule.

I am a little mouse.

I am a little minnow.

I am a little moth.

I am a little mole.

I am a little moose.
Am I little?

Think, Talk, and Write

1. What do you do with your friends? **Text to Self**

2. Which is a character from *Smash! Crash!?* **Character**

3. Look back and write.

Common Core State Standards
Speaking/Listening 1.a. Follow agreed-upon rules for discussions (e.g., listening to others and taking turns speaking about the topics and texts under discussion). Also Speaking/Listening 6., Language 6.

Let's Learn It!

Vocabulary
- Talk about the pictures.
- Put your hand up . . . now down.
- Put your hand in your pocket. Now take it out.

Listening and Speaking
- Make an announcement.
- Listen to a classmate's message or announcement.
- Retell or summarize your classmate's message or announcement.

Vocabulary

Position Words

in

out

up

down

Listening and Speaking

Announcements/Messages

Be a good speaker!

Common Core State Standards

Literature 1. With prompting and support, ask and answer questions about key details in a text. **Also Literature 3., 7.**

At a Farmer's Market

Let's Practice It!

Signs

- Listen to the selection.
- What is the selection about?
- Point to each sign. Tell what it means.
- Why does each stand at the market have a sign? Who will read the signs?
- How do the signs help Sandra with her plans?

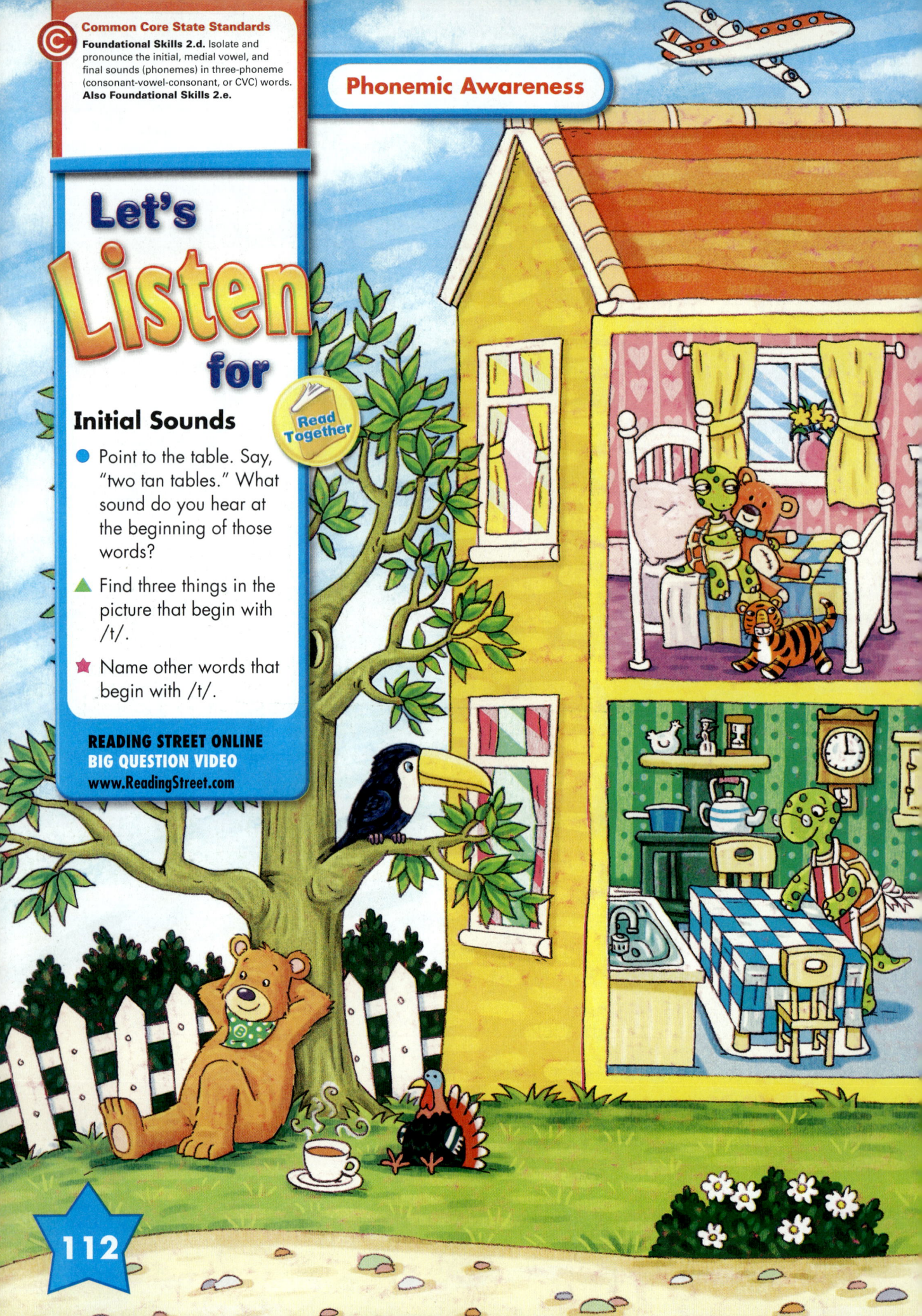

Common Core State Standards
Foundational Skills 2.d. Isolate and pronounce the initial, medial vowel, and final sounds (phonemes) in three-phoneme (consonant-vowel-consonant, or CVC) words. Also Foundational Skills 2.e.

Phonemic Awareness

Let's Listen for

Initial Sounds

- Point to the table. Say, "two tan tables." What sound do you hear at the beginning of those words?
- Find three things in the picture that begin with /t/.
- Name other words that begin with /t/.

READING STREET ONLINE
BIG QUESTION VIDEO
www.ReadingStreet.com

Read Together

Common Core State Standards
Language 5.a. Sort common objects into categories (e.g., shapes, foods) to gain a sense of the concepts the categories represent.

Comprehension

Envision It!
Classify and Categorize

**READING STREET ONLINE
ENVISION IT! ANIMATIONS**
www.ReadingStreet.com

Common Core State Standards
Foundational Skills 2.c. Blend and segment onsets and rimes of single-syllable spoken words.
Also Foundational Skills 3.a., 3.c.

Mm

motorcycle

Tt

turtle

READING STREET ONLINE
ALPHABET CARDS
www.ReadingStreet.com

Phonics
Initial *m*, Initial *t*

Letter Sounds I Know

M m   M m

T t   T t

High-Frequency Words

Words I Can Read

to

a

Sentences I Can Read

1. I am a little  .

2. I 🏃 to 🏫 .

Common Core State Standards
Foundational Skills 4. Read emergent-reader texts with purpose and understanding.
Also Foundational Skills 3.a., 3.c.

Phonics

Decodable Reader

- Consonant Tt (with rebus)
  tiger
  turtle
  turkey
  toad
  toucan
  tadpole

- High-Frequency Words
  I
  to
  a

▲ Read the story.

**READING STREET ONLINE
DECODABLE eREADERS**
www.ReadingStreet.com

Let's Go

Written by Liz Cristie
Illustrated by Larry Jordon

Decodable Reader 6

I walk to a tiger.

I walk to a turtle.

I walk to a turkey.

I walk to a toad.

I walk to a toucan.

I walk to a tadpole.

I walk home.

Think, Talk, and Write

1. How are the trucks in *Smash! Crash!* and *Dig Dig Digging* different?

   Text to Text

2. Which things belong together? Classify and Categorize

3. Look back and write.

Common Core State Standards
Speaking/Listening 4. Describe familiar people, places, things, and events and, with prompting and support, provide additional detail. Also Speaking/Listening 1.a., Language 5.a., 5.c., 6.

Let's Learn It!

Vocabulary
- Talk about the pictures.
- What do you see that is big? What is little?
- Who is tall and who is short?

Listening and Speaking
- Where do AlphaBuddy's stories take place?

Vocabulary
Words for Sizes

big

little

tall

short

128

Listening and Speaking

Respond to Literature
Drama

Be a good listener!

Common Core State Standards

Literature 1. With prompting and support, ask and answer questions about key details in a text. **Also Literature 5.**

Let's Practice It!

Folk Tale

- Listen to the folk tale.
- What can you tell about the third little pig?
- What does the wolf say each time he comes to a house?
- What lesson do the first two pigs learn?
- Why do people like to read or listen to this story?

The Three Little Pigs

Pictionary

Words for Things That Go

airplane

bike

truck

car

bus

van

boat

train

Words for Colors

Pictionary

Words for Shapes

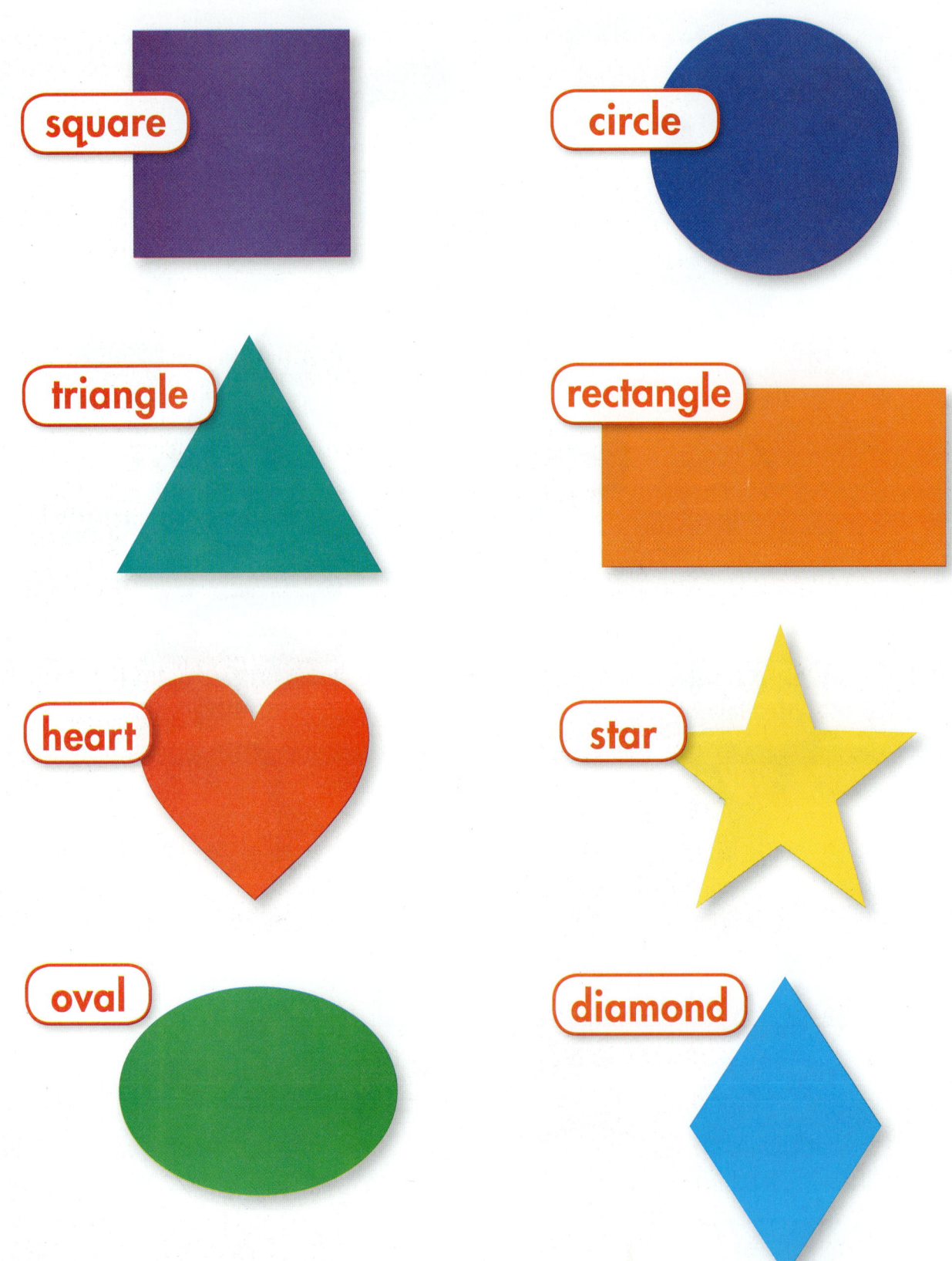

134

Words for Places

school

home

park

train station

police station

fire station

post office

library

Pictionary

Words for Animals

136

butterfly

fish

whale

caterpillar

bear

panda

beaver

calf

cow

Pictionary

Words for Actions

skip

walk

run

fly

swim

ride

jump

hop

Position Words

Pictionary

Words for Feelings

happy

frightened

worried

excited

angry

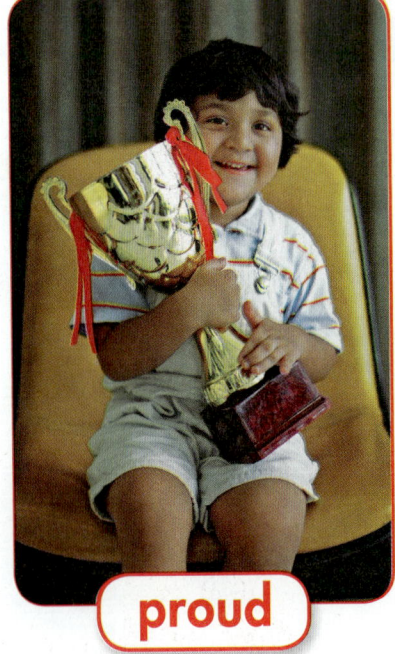
proud

sad

surprised

Acknowledgments

Illustrations
Cover: Rob Hefferan
12 Manja Stojic
19–25 Maria Mola
30–31 C. B. Canga
32 Stephen Lewis
39–45 Cale Atkinson
48, 89, 108–110 Mick Reid
52 Ariel Pang
59–65 Natalia Vasquez
70–71 Akemi Gutierrez
72 Amanda Haley
79–85 Robbie Short
92 Ken Wilson Max
112 Jamie Smith
119–125 Dani Jones
130–131 John Ashton Golden

Photographs
Photo locators denoted as follows: Top (T), Center (C), Bottom (B), Left (L), Right (R), Background (Bkgd)

10 (B) ©Michael Keller/Corbis
16 GRIN/NASA
28 ©Drive Images/Alamy Images, ©Lew Robertson/Corbis, ©Motoring Picture Library/Alamy Images, Getty Images
29 ©Alan Schein Photography/Corbis, ©Ron Chapple/Corbis
36 ©JLV Image Works/Fotolia; ©Duncan Noakes/Fotolia; ©théos/Fotolia; ©acmanley/Fotolia; ©Dmitry_saparov/Fotolia; ©mario beauregard/Fotolia
47 ©Corbis/AGE Fotostock
56 ©Mat Hayward/Fotolia; ©daphot75/Fotolia; ©idelfoto/Fotolia
76 ©Fyle/Fotolia; ©lioneldivepix/Fotolia; ©glucches/Fotolia
86 (T, C) Jupiter Images
88 ©Andersen Ross/Blend Images/Corbis, ©Derrick Alderman/Alamy Images, ©Ellen Isaacs/Alamy Images, Corbis/Jupiter Images
96 ©François Eric/Fotolia
109 ©Jim Craigmyle/Corbis, ©Peter Christopher/Masterfile Corporation
116 Andreas Schlegel/Getty Images
127 (C) ©DK Images, (T) Getty Images
128 Corbis/Jupiter Images, Jupiter Images
129 ©ImageState/Alamy Images, ©Ron Buskirk/Alamy Images, Jupiter Images
132 (CR) ©Basement Stock/Alamy, (TR, TL, TC, BL) Getty Images
133 (B) Getty Images
135 (BCL) ©Guillen Photography/Alamy Images, (BCR) ©Kinn Deacon/Alamy Images, (BR) Flavio Beltran/Shutterstock, (TCR) Photos to Go/Photolibrary
136 (BR) ©Arthur Morris/Corbis, (CC) ©Cyril Laubscher/DK Images, (TL) ©Dave King/DK Images, (BC) ©Gordon Clayton/DK Images, (CR) ©Karl Shone/DK Images, (CL) ©Marc Henrie/DK Images, (TR) DK Images, (TC, BCL) Getty Images, (BL) Jane Burton/(c)DK Images
137 (CR) ©A. Ramey/PhotoEdit, ©Comstock Images/Jupiter Images, (CL) ©Cyndy Black/Robert Harding World Imagery, (CC) ©Dave King/DK Images, (BR, BC) ©Gordon Clayton/DK Images, ©Rudi Von Briel/PhotoEdit, (TC, BL) Getty Images
138 (TR) ©Rubberball Productions, (BR) Jupiter Images, (TL) Photodisc/Thinkstock/Getty Images, (BC) Photos to Go/Photolibrary, (TC) Steve Shott/©DK Images
139 (TR, TC) ©Max Oppenheim/Getty Images, (CR, BR) Getty Images, (C, BL) Rubberball Productions
142 (CR) ©Pete Pahham/Fotolia, (BL) ©Simon Marcus/Corbis, (TR, TL) Getty Images, (TC) Jupiter Images, (C) Photos to Go/Photolibrary, (BR) Rubberball Productions